Jezebel's Kiss

An intimate & spiritual guide in avoiding relationship mistakes

Ricky Boone

Andrea Johnson Books Publishing

Other Books by Ricky Boone

Pillow Talk

Juice Box

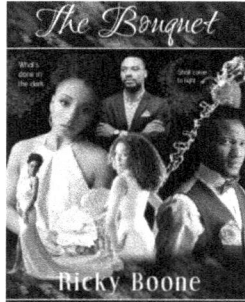

The Bouquet

To learn more about Ricky Boone and his upcoming books, visit the publishing website at: www.Ajbpublishing.com

First published by Andrea Johnson Books Publishing. 2/22/2024

6565 N. MacArthur Blvd, Suite 225 Dallas, TX. 75039
www.Ajbpublishing.com

ISBN: 979-8-9861662-2-3

*I dedicate this book to **Ira Jean Lewis**, my loving grandmother and faithful woman of God*

- Ricky Boone

Acknowledgements

I would like to thank those who played a big part in the experience that gave me the knowledge and wisdom behind this book and all the hell in my life, and friends with their stories.

My beautiful wife Nowealla Boone and Grandmother Ira Lewis who helped me figure how to make this thing into a positive inspirational write.

Diana Buford, Crystal Palasek, Shani Brown, Eric Bryant who is one of my most influential cousins.

But I mainly would like to acknowledge my Wife who has shown me what a real woman is supposed to be and look like, and my grandmother who has shown me how to recognize what's real and what's not. The woman who has told me 100s of times about these red flags and no goods and how to seek a Godly woman and how to recognize real love. She is a true woman of Wisdom.

Ricky Boone

Jezebel's Kiss

They say life and death is in the power of the tongue, which I truly believe, because whatever you feed the mind emerges into the heart and whatever you feed into the heart, goes into the soul, and feeds the soul.

Whatever feeds the soul pretty much comes out of the mouth, which is manifestation. A lot of our crazy situation is based on words spoken. Many of us are in these crazy situations based on what is spoken into existence, and it has a lot to do with the way we think. (Proverbs 23: So as a man thinketh in his heart so is he)

However, if you think you are a loser, and you believe he just wants to place his seed in you, you will never get married, you will never prosper, and you won't change the whole mindset. How you view things or how you see yourself, or how far you will go.

Throughout my life I've done all these things the hard way. Whether it was relationships or friendships or even something as simple as being on a job. Words have power, which is what we give to others that we claim to love. A person shouldn't know we have that type of power, to be able to control your emotions or your actions, your wheel. God is the only one that should have that type of control.

The mind is a terrible thing to waste, especially if you give it to someone who is a manipulator or control freak. People like this show no value in you, but only in themselves. They'll mess up in some way and somehow find a way to place the blame on you, but not recognize their own personal faults, and if you're not wise a lot of times, you'll fall for it.

I knew a woman one time that was having problems within her relationship. They were on and off for about five years. The guy was very jealous, she couldn't even say hi or even have male friends without him thinking she has some type of emotional or sexual relationship with them.

He would mentally and physically abuse her, and to the point one day she actually left for the third time. However, he begged and begged her back saying sorry in so many different ways, to the point she actually came back because he said he was going to change.

Newsflash, he never did. She got so comfortable with him she finally said; I understand him, in other words she settled.

Newsflash, you don't have to settle for anything that doesn't allow you to feel secure and comfortable. No one should want to be in a relationship that makes them feel like they're walking on eggshells. This thing is also a 50-50 give-and-take movement, you shouldn't have to give up anything if he or she isn't giving up anything. And if it isn't any agreement, it's best to part and find yourself a better fit and learn to love yourself more.

There are five things you must always remember:

1 loving you should be the first priority.

2 take care of home is next.

3 recognize the little things due to most times those are the most important things.

4 If you take care of her or him, they'll take care of you.

5 But maybe this one should've been number one: make sure you keep God first in all things that you do.

Love is the most important thing out of them all.

Love is not complicated, love is not control, love is not confusion, loves does not manipulate, love is God.

And if there's a person that you're with that does not share the same or value the same principles, you don't need to be with them. Because being unequally yoked, man, is something that you do not want to face.

Being with somebody that does not share the same love with the same value or the same beliefs, such as yourself.

Because if a person does not know and love God, how can they love you? God is perfect love, if that man has a relationship with God and loves God, he can surely love you correctly. Try falling in love or should I say, growing in love with a man or a woman who truly loves God. God will bless you with someone who will love you full-time instead of part-time, as long as your love in him is full time.

Who wants to be with someone that's seasonal instead of permanent? That's what we must learn to recognize, who are seasonal and who are permanent people in our lives. We could fall in love with someone who is meant to be seasonal, but we make them permanent and wonder why they exit out our lives so easily so quick and so fast, because it wasn't love.

This happens to many of us, we will be seeking love, will be so busy trying to fall in love instead of trying to grow in life. I would Vow never to fall in love again, or that's what I used to say, due to just as fast as you can fall in love, you can fall out of love even faster.

One thing I can say, never allow yourself to change to fit anyone else's lifestyle. You change it because you wanted to change it for yourself, not for someone else. Or you forfeit and end up going back to being whatever you were comfortable being, and they will most definitely go back to being whatever the heck they were meant to be, even if it was a hoe.

SEEK ,SEARCH, CHOSEN

A lot of women and men's problem today is that they can't stay still, they want a woman or a man now, so they go out looking and searching and seeking, instead of just sitting or standing still and maintaining. They will get up and get dressed, head to the clubs, the church, the parks, the grocery store or whatever it takes to seek. Most times they are very vulnerable, and when I see these things in the end, I find something that causes them to be insecure and causes them to be vulnerable, and they overlook the red flags.

The Bible says he that seeks and finds a wife, finds a good thing, not she that finds a husband finds a good thing. A lot of women don't know their position. Which explains why we have all these unequally yoked relationships and dysfunctional relationships, because we move out of lust and we act like we are so in need.

One of the main reasons why I didn't want to be in relationships is that we act like we lonely, we don't know why we really want a relationship. A relationship should be based on God, which is number one. Number two is the quality, meaning strength from a man. This is how a man can bring security and how he handles things in a relationship, setting the tone when the woman wants control.

Number three is support, being able to talk out things, being able to communicate and know you're open to tell them the truth about what you observed. Being positive is number four, this is very important in how you handle a frustrating situation and showing that love. Number five is confidence. Know what she wants, likes and needs. Take the time to really know her, know how to approach her and value her.

Number six is stepping up. Knowing when to come and take over and knowing when to shut it down. These are some of the qualities you must have. Also, a lot of the women accept a man-child, which is men that refuses to grow up and they still have boyish ways.

These are some of the things a woman needs to look forward to in a man, especially when that man is calling himself seeking her. But the main thing she should want in a man, is a man of his word. Stick to what you say you're going to do and do it. And last but not least, is affection.

Your woman shouldn't have to remind you to kiss and hold her and touch her and tell her how beautiful she is. In love and affection within the relationship, show her you love her, it's the little things that matter.

hold her hand, open up doors, pull out the chair for her. If you have a problem doing these things you have a problem with yourself, and you could be the reason why she's bouncing and repeating cycles and your bouncing repeating your cycles as well.

Always remember, this love does not keep you together, what keeps you together is God. Don't allow people to talk you into being in a situation that just won't work. If that person has issues with keeping themselves and forcing themselves to be with you, it'll never work. You can't make somebody into something that's just not in them.

There used to be an old saying that said; you can't lead a horse to water and make them drink it. In other words, you can't make somebody love you and you can't turn a hoe into a housewife. In some factors it is possible, but in some sense sometimes people just won't change and it's just them. The same way you'll find a person, most likely it a be the same way they'll be, when they walk away from you.

Don't expect people to change based on how you treat them. You can treat them like gold but eventually the transition of them being everything and anything *that you want will happen, but eventually again they'll go back to being exactly who they are and what they are comfortable being. And most likely it a be what their known for which is a hoe.*

The bible covers 24:3 by wisdom and understanding. That scripture means it's a nice place to be all the time, marrying him or her because you want to be there. But have wisdom and strength and knowledge. Knowledge is information which is what the scripture is talking about, in order to keep this relationship. Prayer does not cancel ignorance, you have to learn and have to study this.

If someone ever tells you that they love you, ask them how much do they know about you?

The next one is understanding. Mini comprehension upon understanding and wisdom, is application. Meaning you cannot apply what you don't understand, and you cannot understand what you don't know.

We don't want to continue to keep living our lives in and out of relationships that we seem to never understand. Now we're old and full of wisdom, we should understand and know when we get into situations how to bail out.

When we are old, we are full of wisdom or should I say full of regret. Which is crazy because regret is nothing but experience. We wish we never had shooters original information, which is from the source. And the guy that caught some self-truth, he is basically saying he is the source, the original information.

You don't wanna be in love with a fool or a fool in love. Get to know the individual, don't pour out all your heart so quick to the point you're giving him or her free game, meaning they transition into being everything you want, but in reality, they could be really everything you despise.

Let a person figure you out, you don't have to spill the beans and tell him everything about your past, because the very second you tell them about your past you give them energy, and you also give them a weapon to use against you. They're going to start comparing themselves by everything that you went through. Everybody you've been through, and most likely play like they're the opposite, but sometimes mainly be the same way the person you was with before, having the same spirit as them. Stay the hell away from them.

I try to look at myself as an accomplished writer, a king, a man of integrity, different. God created me totally different from others in the way that I think is not like no other. I spoke things into existence into myself. I had to just because of the things that I've seen and the things that was around me and the things that I've been through. Meaning I was exposed at an early age to things that I wasn't supposed to see, things before my time, if people only knew.

This is what made me into the man I am today. I learned that people are going to do what they are going to do, regardless of the situation. It made me not insecure, but it made me realize we are only human and that the same way you find them, is the same way they're going to walk away from you. The same way you pick them up, most likely will be the same way you lose them.

I once met a woman who was in a relationship who had a man, but at the same time we were friends. She saw me pretty much occupied with another woman, but at the same time she was going through issues with her own relationship. We both used to share each other's feelings towards the relationship that we were in, but once I started showing interest in her, she found a way to walk into my life and she dropped the guy like a bad habit. Came up with many excuses on why she walked away from him. He didn't have a job, he didn't want to get a job, he's so weird.

Everything she used to so-called love so much about him, all of a sudden became weird, as she took an interest in me and so forth. Once the truth talks your eyes open, and you see how much people play off your emotions, people play off your emotions only due to their own hurts and lack of self-esteem, which is number one. I truly believe the only reason men and women are insecure to a good woman or a good man, it's only because the lack of them not being able to live up to expectations.

This particular woman played off my emotions. I was very vulnerable; I was also seeking love, but at the same time I was trying to mend something back together that was meant to stay broken.

She came back with tears in her eyes, I swear if she was nominated for an Oscar she would win. I instantly fell for it. In the spiritual realm we call this the spirit of Jezebel. A manipulating and controlling spirit. She controlled me with every bit of poison you can possibly think of. It was mainly sex; we would call this type a *nympho. She was very experienced in a lot of sexual acts That I wasn't. I could no longer see myself and see how I was acting and see how I was moving. My whole thought process was completely changed. I didn't even know what made me the man I once was. I knew nothing about myself, only thing I could think of was making this person happy. It was a controlling spirit that had me so out of my mind, it was a very dominant spirit.*

You have to view life as it is and say to yourself are you going to go through it, or are you going to grow through it? You need to learn to expect things to get better things, it will pass for you, and you will come out the situation. But in my case, it was a little bit crazy for me to come out of that situation, because I was so comfortable in the situation and even though you would think you can change it, it's not that simple.

You can't, it's impossible for you to change because it's not your job to change the situation, because you can't change the person, no matter how good the sex is, or how good you sex them. That's the only thing that they're programmed to. Because you can't change their mind, meaning you can't change the spirit so whatever's been locked into their spirit causes them to be comfortable, and is in their soul and whatever's in their soul is in their heart, so it's impossible. But not for God to change, but it is for you.

I never thought that things would get better. I was a 30-year-old stuck with the mindset of a 20-year-old. Understand this, whatever happens, acting as a 20-year-old separates you from your future.

I was stuck thinking with the wrong head, getting head. The devil had my mind twisted and folded. I didn't know what to do, I was soul tied to a demon. So just imagine being soul tied to a person that had many spirits, and unfamiliar spirits tied off into them. So all those demons, those sex demons in them now had me and my mind, and I began to now think like a hoe.

Now before I started acting out what I was thinking, my mind set started planning. I started targeting certain women, I started planning out things that you wouldn't imagine, I started asking questions.

I started being curious when women would talk to me, I would be everything that they would want in a man. Pretty much the same way the woman that put all her spirits into me, that sucked the soul out of me and out my sleep, that taunted my dreams ...I was now her; we were one.

First and foremost, you must break a hold and release yourself from that strong hold, because whenever you are softened to the person, that man or woman is now off in you. You begin to pick up their habits. Deliverance must take place before you even allow yourself to move on, or you will carry the next baggage of things onto the next.

You must first learn to clear your mind from the baggage that has happened to you in your life, declare War on whatever's hindering you and that has possibly happened in your life. Because nothing is permanent, not even marriage. Relationships, loved ones, everyone and everything must die. Time determines everything. Whatever you invest in your time is what you become. There are people in your life that you need to drop, because they're taking up too much of your time and time is everything.

Never allow your emotions to control you, learn to discipline your emotions, weeds don't have to have any encouragement to grow. Your mind goes on automatic; you don't have to water weeds or give them water or sunshine to grow, weeds will grow through the cracks of the sidewalk by themselves.

However, to grow roses or other exotic flowers they're special steps you must take in order for them to grow properly. Just like us we take steps in life, you don't have to beat yourself up or hate someone to grow. No need for bitterness or to stress your mind, our minds are placed on this thing called automatic. Let's get straight to the point, the mind will be willing to do all these things itself, but in order to move into your greatness, you gotta be willing to humble yourself and suffer. But don't sleep, still act and push and go on because this hell you go through doesn't last forever, only to those who allow themselves to stay stuck.

In time in other words, don't listen to what the devil deals with, because ignorance is in our nature, but it can be broken. However, this is what a lot of us deal with when we lack understanding. We then try to force the fact and don't want to accept the truth. That we can't change people and they won't change. This is all lies that we face within ourselves, we don't wanna face the truth. It was written when the devil speak lies, he speaks his own native tongue. If I lie, in other words.

For example, have you ever lied so much to the point that you start believing in your own actualization? To the point you lied so much that your lie actually became the truth, but it became the truth only to you. Sad case right? In other words, everything around you would be false, because that's what you fed on lies, so in other words you thinking and claiming you love someone could possibly be a lie. Your pain lied to you, and you could be caught up and lost. That is what causes a lot of our hearts to be broken. You can post on social media, portraying to be in love with someone for years, but they're in lust with you. People eventually find themselves. Like I always say, do you love what you do for them? Or is it the thought of being in love with them? But people can be so insecure that you're really just so vulnerable and in lust.

Growing up I learned a lot of things, you know, especially from my mother. She always told me the same way you get them, be the same when you lose them. I found that kind a hard to be true at first, but I ended up meeting that woman.

I met a woman that pretty much was like everything that I always thought she would be. She would cook, she would clean, sex me everywhere and anywhere and it was like you know I had to sit back and think, how did she even come to be in existence with me? Because at first she had a man, and her man wasn't trying to get a job, or do all the things that she wanted. So I never Intervened in her relationship. Until one day I suddenly started to ignore her, stopped calling, stopped showing that I was pressed. I did all those things and eventually she kept blowing my phone up. Asking suddenly, are you at home? Can you have company? Do you want company? Sure, why not? Which is what I replied. She came over and picked me up, took me over to a friend's house.

Who later on about six, seven to eight years, I was with her. It was eight years I ended up with, I eventually ended up with both women. I married one and divorced the other. Turned around and married her friend, it was a messy situation. It was all because I was bitter, and I was hurt. I was ignorant, I was stubborn. But if you really wanna look at it, it was all the spirits that was in her as well as the woman before her in me.

Because everything that they've done to me, I turned around and did it 2 to 3 times worse to them. I actually had all three of them all in the same week, which is the craziest thing I can honestly say that I've ever done.

the mindset of a hoe, that's exactly what I was. A whore with a whole bunch of unfamiliar spirits in me.

But back to the woman that I said I met, that picked me up and took me to a friend's house. She dropped her guy within a month or two of the relationship, prior to coming over to see me. Anyway, we would kiss, and we talked. We talked about the craziest things but we would never have sex with one another. But the very second she dropped him like a bad habit, she came to pick me up that night and that's when we first slept with each other. And the things that I experienced with this woman, were things that I've never experienced before within the 15 years prior to the woman I was with. I thought I did everything You could think of to a woman, but apparently, I didn't.

I was wicked totally sprung to the point that I had to have her at least 3,4,5 times a day it was crazy. I seen and felt myself begin to change to the point I started to think like her, move like her, speak like her. Sex stayed on my mind. Pornos became almost like an everyday thing because she was a porn fanatic. We would sit up and watch a whole porn like a movie and eat dinner and popcorn, sometime have sex while watching a porn, it was crazy.

This woman I could not let go, even though we were broken up, months later we ended up back in each other's bed. We would break up again close to a year, and months later we ended up back in each other's bed again. This is how the tie kept us joined together, we became one.

Her bad habits became my bad habits. I started smoking cigarettes, I started doing everything that It took to keep her in my circle. It had gotten to the point that I even got back to smoking weed, it was crazy. It was like a total control over me, this is what you would call the spirit of Jezebel.

Jezebel Spirit

Well to start off, the Jezebel spirit is a manipulating controlling spirit. It's either their way or no way, if you don't do what they say, they gonna walk out of your life. Tantrums are thrown, and they're quick to get frustrated with everything. It's almost like they have split personalities. The Bible says a double minded person is unstable in all his ways, in this case I was the one that was unstable. But I was being controlled by this off of my spirit that I couldn't break loose from.

The power of sex is crazy, I mean once you get a hold to it or they get a hold to you, it's like a whole personality. Your whole character changes, you constantly pick up that person's whole swag, whether you were a thief a liar and a whore, or whatever issue I had. They may have it as well and it becomes yours.

But this Jezebel spirit, it was like; get out my house, or do what I say. I was so pressed not knowing I was locked in. She would use methods like; if you don't like the way I think get out, well this is not your house anyway if you don't like the way I talk and the way that I sound get out, and if you don't like the way I pray and look and the way that I do things get out. But the very second I would fall victim to it, and submit, everything will turn back into normal and we end up in a cycle again, sex sex sex. It was almost as if I was a puddle, if you know what I mean, like I had a spill up on me. Because I would come home and be depressed, and she would know exactly what to do to relieve my stress. When she came home depressed, I didn't know what to do, I would give her sex, weed or whatever, but not knowing she was talking to somebody else and I wasn't the only one that had this tie.

You know in the beginning everything was perfect, you say all the right things to do all the right things. The smiles in the morning, the nice talks, back rubs, all those things calm you, and it's like everything is perfect. But then all of a sudden you will wake up one day and then there's a lock on the phone, then there's no food cooked, then he doesn't want to go to work, and she doesn't wanna have sex. And he doesn't want to cut the grass and she doesn't wanna wash the dishes. It becomes like everything that you see one said that they would do, those things don't exist anymore.

It's almost like they did everything they could possibly do to get you and now that they got you, they gone back to their normal self. As if they transition their lies over to fit your life. Crazy to put out that much energy, to go that far. It's almost like as if he, you, me ...was just an experience or experiment.

People can be so stubborn sometimes, meaning they really don't want somebody else to have you. It's like oh I wonder how it is to be with that person, to the point you probably been ignored for years, months. They never really paid you any attention, until somebody else caught your attention.

When I was younger, I was in a relationship very short term. You know I was kicking it with her. She was a very good woman, she was studying to be a nurse she had a head on the shoulders she had everything going for herself. But it was something that was about the spirit that kept drawing me back, I mean actually she gave me a second chance because I ditched her for the woman before. The crazy thing about it was that we were both in a process of getting a divorce. I got my divorce first she got a divorce second, but at the time we both were still married, I got married in a month she got married in the same month, but 14 days later.

We both had a lot in common, we had goals we had dreams, but we also had sexual desires. She was also experienced as well, even though she was a little younger, but the spirit that was off in me was very curious.

Curious to teach her what I have learned from the last woman I was with. I was determined to turn this chick out, flip her inside out, sideways, backwards, whatever it was I can put to play. It was about to happen with this woman, due to the desires that was in me. They was like a burning flame, I had to release it and I had to release it fast, and whatever was in me, I was about to put off into her.

I often wondered if the last love I was with thought the same thing. Almost like even though we was away from each other, did she think about me at the very same time I thought about her, crazy how that spirit can connect.

It's crazy how whenever I found myself out of a relationship, I was back with her. That control was a Jezebel spirit. No, I'm not saying that she was a Jezebel, I'm saying the spirit that dwells in her that used her, was that spirit. Because we will often have conversations like; did you think about me while I was away? And she would often tell me she did. She even used to masturbate to my pictures, and think about me at the same time she was laying with another.

Crazy how that spirit works, but then again, I was back in the bed being controlled. Following her every move. She get hers, I get mine, she want sex, I want sex. She hungry, I'm hungry. I was like a puppy being controlled. She was controlling me while I was controlling others. It was like when she was done with me, I was back on the prowl calling girls from off of Facebook: old exes turning them out, doing all kinds of crazy things, feedin their spirit with mine. These were the thoughts I was having, dealing with the spirit of Jezebel.

I was the manipulating king. I knew how to make people feel sorry for me, I knew how to make people want me. I knew how to make people hate me, to get what I want to make people like me and love me. To get what I want I was a certified hoe, a certified gigolo. I would get money, I would get plenty of sex, I would get conversation, but most of all I would get you, so I would tie into you to the point I would make you addicted to me. I would make you want me, even if you didn't like me. These are the spirits that I had. The spirit of Jezebel.

The Jezebel spirit is a Minnesota spirit, it's a dominating and controlling spirit. I mean this woman pretty much got away with everything that she wanted concerning me, by threatening me, by using the spirit of fear. And if anybody has to use fear against you to make you move, it is most definitely not of God. But she threatened to end our relationship, she's threatened to do all sorts of things that caused damage to the relationship, and the love we supposedly had. I feared losing her.

The Jezebel spirit does not only work through sex and relationships. It also can be worked in the church through controlling. If somebody does not understand you, and if you don't learn to move and agree with everything that they put out, they will use force with it or use fear with it. Or because you don't agree with their teachings, we're not following them and if you don't move the way that they move concerning whatever, it would be a lot of this stuff that takes place even in the choir. I've seen people argue and fight over songs that they feel should only be sung, due to they be intimidated by others because they sing better, so they use control and manipulation to make that person feel uncomfortable.

Manipulation, well it's something we are almost too accustomed to in the beginning of a relationship. You must set sexual boundaries or what you will tolerate, and what you will not tolerate and to be honest with each other. You never wanna chase. There's a difference between chasing and pursuing a person. There's a thin line between desire and desperation. You cannot be so desperate so it will say thirsty, it can cause you to lose respect and could be very unattractive. Doesn't it make you feel as if you are one of the options? Being desperate leads to how you start, it's how you finish your finals of making more of an effort to make it work. While the other hoes sit back and wait, you'll find yourself burnt out. I hope to be like super 50-50 to build something amazing, that manipulation would never step in. If you ever find yourself chasing, think of these things:

1 they might not be all that interested.

2 they go on the defense.

3 or real feelings aren't possibly there.

4 or maybe they just want to feel good about herself or himself due to the low self-esteem.

Always remember you can't change anybody; they have to be willing to heal themselves or you're looking at a total disaster. And when a person pulls away, excuses become actions. Behavior changes. Take heed to the test dealing with the attention needed. When a person doesn't really know what's going on with you, he or she is curious, but the second she figured or he figured you out, they don't care. Especially when they now gotcha, you can't confess your feelings to someone who doesn't value you or care at all about your feelings.

Manipulation is basically waiting to take its course. You find yourself thinking you was the fool, certain people can make you feel as if the whole crash of the relationship was your fault.

Never find yourself in a position that you are so used to having certain things, to the point you now lack understanding. Don't sell out because you're so used to having what they offered you. Step back and think outside the box. What if you lose whatever it is you have now? And this was that very moment you lost it. What would you do? Where would you go?

People with these types of scars, and dealing with people that have the Jezebel spirit are hard to deal with. Because they are now insecure, you can't fault the new person for what the last person has done to you. Because then a light switch clicks on and the very person that was for you, you boxed in and now you've dumped all that baggage on to them.

What I learned which is a fact, is when you stop chasing that's when people start caring. And when you stop looking and start working and loving yourself, people start noticing you, so just be yourself. Sometimes you have to fall back in order to get it, get the attention that you need from the person you actually love. And sometimes you'll be a fool doing just that.

Some people enjoy the excitement with the thrill, especially when it comes to a woman. Some women value excitement, doing what they want, especially when you're showing that you care too much. Be careful because some women can be so savage, almost as if they are a man, because it's in a man's nature to be a savage dog. We do doggish things as if it's natural to us, but when a woman does it it's dangerous. You won't expect it, its crafty and actually they move smarter than us as well.

Some women are actually waiting and looking for that man to save them, just like some weak men are looking for some women to save them. Like J Cole said: (she don't wanna be saved) don't waste your time trying to save them, save yourself, don't hold your breath, keep living. Some women all they value is the money, and the sex that secures them.

However some of those dumb men out there loves to flash and pull out money, just to show them what they have. I call them attention seekers, and we wonder why all she wants is money, but at the same time here we go again. The same way you market yourself, you put yourself out there, is what you gonna attract. You are what you attract. You can't expect to get a Morris chestnut and you carry yourself like Cardi B. You can't expect to get a Nia Long and you carry yourself like Kodak Black. It's just a mix sometimes that just doesn't work, and if it does work that's like the oddest couple ever. It's got to be mentality and chemistry, that's just my opinion, not money. But love has no face, neither does booty.

Overall stop showing people that you care so much about people that don't care about you. Stop showing that you care, it's all about the moment. He or she could be in love with the moment of having you, the thrill of having you.

When you fall back from them, they'll begin to crave you because they can't have you, and the urge to crave somebody hmmm...It's like the most explosive orgasm that you could ever have. Notice that when you lust, or should I say touch, in other words something that you have no business touching, it be the most exciting moment of your life. It's like the best sex in the world, only because it's a forbidden fruit. Or it's something that you shouldn't have, it's really off-limits to touch and to taste.

Always remember that people are good for the body but can be damaging to the soul. Keep your mind guarded but open, just like the options god presented. A lot of people stay stuck in the situation due to their mindsets. They are in their comfort zone, we must get out of that comfort zone.

Think like a hoe

Please understand sometimes people just don't change, it may not be meant for them to change with you. Some people are brought into our lives for a season, and we make them permanent. Always remember that enough is enough.

Guard your mind, don't allow people to waste your time and let time pass by you and you miss your blessings. Our minds say no, this isn't good for you, but the heart has you fooled into believing that people can be helped. Me myself, I was a victim to this type of situation.

This is what we want in relationship builders.

One cannot build while the other stands and watch, trust me if he or she is gonna stand and watch you build, they are temporary, it won't last so why waste your time?

Let's talk about patience, which is the only way to learn and understand. It is when you have to use it. You don't learn patience from people of the church, you learn patience when God causes you to fall into what we call a season. Where you have to exercise it, and

41

pretty much almost go crazy. These situations that God places you in is when you don't have a choice but to wait, and most time the decisions we make we place our ourselves in. Patience isn't about if you wait, but how you wait. It is a trait that God wants to build in the inside of builders. And a lot of us may not understand this because we are runners, we give up too fast to even watch the manifestation take place once we wait.

God builds in the builder, before the builder creates things. In other words, he draws out the blueprint and places it in us, strengthening us to build it. This is what we want in the relationship, to build us. One cannot build while the other stands still to watch.

What's most important is that we must learn to grow in love, rather than fall in love. Or we might be falling in love with the wrong thing or wrong person that does not know love at all, just lust. And you'll be falling in love with the booty and money rather than the heart.

Because a hoe has no patience, they want what they want when they want and how they want it. And will say and do anything to get it. Don't get it twisted, a hoe can be a person you don't even have to sleep with. Anybody. It's the mentality that makes that person a hoe. You don't have to be a female, you don't have to be a male, you can have hoe tendencies. To me I look at it like this, a hoe is always trying to get over on somebody. Especially if it's beneficial to them. They care nothing about anything but themselves and their feelings. It's almost as if they are narcissists. They are split personalities, and when caught in their actions, they play stupid. As if they don't know what you're talking about.

Have you ever been around people that have way more than you do, but they don't like you, don't even wanna breathe the same air that you breathe? They don't like you at all, but they have way more than you do. Think about it. They're in higher positions, have way more money, a greater advantage, but they just can't stand the thought of you.

Then you find yourself questioning yourself, like what did I do to make this person dislike me that much? But in reality, it's not you. That's when you know that there's a blessing on your life, that's when you know that God has something good for you, because they're not mad at you. They don't hate you, they just envy the blessing and want that gift that's hidden inside of you.

They see something in you that you don't see in yourself. So if you were to keep 100 with yourself, and look at it like it's not what you did to them, it's who you are. This is the reason why they dislike you.

An attractive older black woman told me once that she sees and loves the potential in me, and that the devil sees the potential that I have in me as well, and to go get those haters that speak on me some shades because my potential is blinding to them. Value yourself, don't allow people to lynch off of you. Those are the hoes. You have to out think them, not think like them.

They already have a plan once they introduced themselves to you, sometimes their intentions don't be to screw you over, because it was always in them to move naturally. Because that's all they know, is to be a hoe, either they learned it from their daddy, or they learned it from their mother or from the company they've been keeping all these years. The Bible says evil communications corrupt good manners, and I find that to be a prime fact.

Another thing that can ruin a good relationship is to take advice from someone that can't take their own advice. *If their relationship is trash garbage toxic, why take advice from them at all? Somebody that has problems within their relationship and it's toxic, shouldn't be trying to give you any advice, especially If they're not married. And even if they are married and their marriage is toxic, and it's abusive with no structure, who are they to give you advice? And you'll be the fool to accept it.*

I went through this in my second marriage, crazy how a person can take in everything someone else says and not their own spouse. You can be saying the same thing and your spouse takes a deaf ear to what you're saying, but their friends can tell them the exact same thing and they listen. Take heed to those who be in your other half's ear, you will want to guard them due to they just might transition and pick up the other person's spirit.

But you never know in these days, they could be making your lover dislike you because they want you for themselves anyway. It happens. I had a woman tell me everything about the woman I was trying to get back with. She was saying, oh you don't want her, she slept with this many people all at the same time, she slept with married men. I mean, she painted the picture of this woman to be so much of a savage, and even though I knew it, she made it worse to the point I didn't wanna even be back with her. And they were best friends, guess who ended up with the best friend? Me. The one that was telling me all the mess. I started up a relationship with her and we shared stories about my ex all the time.

I said to myself, what in the world did I fall in love with? I'm not going back to her; I mean she threw me a curveball to the point I could never look at me ex the same again. And Now I'm with her best friend and about a whole year later, before I even left, I ended back up with the woman that she was talking down about. This was crazy. I went back to her after we dogged her out verbally. This was a stronghold that I was possessed with that I couldn't let go. The crazy thing about it that was funny, was the two women that were the friends that I ended up with, had so much in common, and of course they would have a lot in common.

Because they were best friends. Funny thing is, after we would have sex, one would give me a high five like wow good job. But when I ended up a year later with her best friend, the other woman, she would give me high-fives as well! And I thought that was weird. Like man, what a coincidence. Best friends, they're both freaks, and they both like to give high-fives after intercourse.

It was like jumping into the next relationship, but it was the same. They were very alike, the only difference was one was business minded, and the other one was a worker. One was very clean and a neat freak, and the other was a savage when it came to keeping a house clean. Both of them were extremely Freakazoid's. In this case I was a hoe. It's like I had an unstable mind. I was confused and the devil is the author of confusion. I was double minded. Like the Bible says, a double minded man is unstable in all his ways. I was double minded, and I thought with the wrong head, all I could think about was who was next that I was going to jump in the bed with.

My next victim I would like to say her name was America. I'm going to use America because I don't want to use her real name. But she was so different. I met her on the media and she was the type that was testing me, pushing my buttons, coming at me as if I was scared of her. Another method of intimidation I would like to say she used.

This woman was off into the stars and the moon and lots of astrology and zodiac signs. And all kinds of crazy stuff. She reminded me of a fortuneteller or some type of witch, but man the first day that I met her, me coming over to her house, she came outside with a blanket wrapped around her from just getting out the shower, with nothing on up under it but some boy shorts, lord. By the way I still had all of these spirits in me, they had my mind thinking like a hoe, I was unstable. I wasn't getting paid to sleep with these women, I was sleeping with them for my own pleasure. I needed to get over the past, get over what had broken me. I needed revenge, I needed to cover up some things. This is what happens when you tie into unfamiliar spirits, controlling spirits.

Everything I went through, I pretty much asked God for. It's like instead of asking for money, I asked for wisdom. And God gave me problems, many problems. To solve them, I asked for strength, and God gave me difficulties to make me strong. I asked for courage to face my fears, and God gave me dangers to overcome them. And when I asked God to show me how to love, he gave me trouble and many people to help along my way.

A lot of things were hard to face. I learned that people rooting for you are not always family. And that everybody that goes to jail isn't a criminal. Just as well as everybody in church is not a Christian. I learned to not put all my trust in people. Because we are liable to make mistakes and fall back, and as well some people just may not care at all.

For instance, I know a particular person who admits to all their faults, but at the same time does nothing about it to fix it. He will tell you he has a problem with other women with cheating, but falls victim into fornication every time, in a cycle. He is very manipulative. He would beg for his woman back, then turn around and do the same thing, then she would put him out the door every time. He then plays on her heart because she actually loves him, these are forms as well. Men can carry the spirit of Jezebel as well.

This in particular spirit is very heavy. If you find a person that throws tantrums, spazzes out all because they cannot get their way, this is a form of manipulation and a form of intimidation. Picture getting caught in the act of cheating, then turn it around playing as if you are the victim and starting the fight.

These are hoe tendencies, especially if it's a man that's actually doing this. Your girlfriend goes through your phone, and finds out that you've been playing around with the same woman that she forgave you from cheating with the first time. Confronts you, you are in denial with it, then she pulls up the evidence on you and boom, cold busted. What's the excuse then? They say what's done in the dark shall be revealed to the light. Sometimes it's almost pointless to cheat, especially if you don't know how. If you're not meant to cheat, what's the point of cheating? If you like many women instead of just one, or many men instead of just one?

Rule number one, if he or she started out with you with no locks on the phone, then all of a sudden you all have locks on the phone and you have no children, red flag. Those are clearly signs, especially if they've already given reasons that they would cheat.

Rule number two, if they didn't start out with you with their phones face flat down and every time they get up they take their phones to the bathroom, all secretive, red flag. Take heed to it. It may not be what it may be, but then again ,what if it is?

Rule number three, sexual partners that are now looked at as friends, they can no longer be friends. Especially if you were now in a relationship because of those old friends. For a while it works and know how you like it, and you know what they like. Eventually they would possibly be the first person that they run back to, if they want to cheat, depending on how cool they are. Especially if they are talking on an everyday basis regularly.

Rule number four, secretive conversations, especially with old sexual partners or old friends that are supposed to be like sisters or like play cousins and play brothers. We are too old for the play sisters and play brothers and fake family members, especially if they had possibly some type of connection. Understand this, they're not blood, it could be a big possibility or an urge for something to happen, if it ain't already happened, take heed to those red flags.

I speak from experience, not saying everybody thinks this way or move this way, but me personally I moved that way at one point in time. I had a play sister, we grew up as we were brother and sister. Mind you we are not blood, our parents were just best friends growing up in school, but when I ended up vulnerable in my situation, things finally happened.

I used to think about it a lot, it was almost as if it was premeditated. I always picture myself, what if me and so-called whoever got along, and we begin to have these crazy conversations that everybody else used to have when we were all together, but alone. However, it finally went down.

We are friends till this day due to our parents been best friends our whole lives, but we can no longer view each other in the same eye as we were when we were kids, because we don't have anything for each other. So therefore, if I'm in a relationship I have no business calling this person whatsoever. Vice versa she have no business calling me whatsoever. Because how would I feel if the person that I'm in a relationship with did the same thing?

But imagine a man that had no morals, no standards, he didn't value anything that he had, and he lost everything in the little that he had. He had a woman that was trying to set up to go to school, she bought them cars, rings, and actually stepped his game up as a man, because sometimes we need a strong woman to stand behind us to make us into the man that we are. Don't get me wrong, I'm the type to say I was a man before I met you. But sometimes to get to the next level, we need a strong woman.

Thinking like a hoe, in other words thinking less of your partner or thinking about nobody else but yourself, means ignorant and selfish. You don't care about nobody else's feelings but yours. You're only out to gain what you can in any way that you can, even if it is backstabbing those that are close to you.

I found myself plenty of times trying to test the waters, but I was just not that dumb to testify. So I ran out of all the women around the time I just had my second divorce. I was 37 and this woman was well over 40, possibly 55. She was well seasoned. I met her off of Facebook and the crazy thing about it was that I've been known her for about seven years before we even met, and when we finally met the first thing she brought to mind was what she wants to do to me. She like young guys and she wanted me to back up Everything that I said I would do.

However, I had vowed never to sleep or mess around with this woman, but just have fun and games, just to see how my talk game was and how I could pull in all the women. But she had other plans.

I don't wanna go too much far over the details, but it started off with just oral sex. Me not giving it, but me receiving it. And trust me it was something that I've never experienced before, because I had a lot of women who know how to perform on me, but they wasn't 50 years old and if I wasn't mistaken, she was trying to suck the soul out of my body.

I had so many sexual encounters not with many women, but with odd, unorthodox women. Pretty much all of them were weird and some type of way and carried some type of spirit that always tied me in. Whenever I got stressed, whenever I got bored, whenever I felt I needed to talk and express my feelings instead of rolling a blunt, I'm gonna pour a bottle of liquor or drink and I would simply call her. And she knew exactly what to do and what I wanted and I would leave relieved.

The door was opened to the point that she started calling me for personal things, like could I bring her a loaf of bread, could I bring her some coffee and could I bring her a Pepsi. It was like as if I was her man. I had to let her know I wasn't that type of person, that I was only out for one thing and that was to get in her pants whenever I felt the need. To be totally honest, I always seem to give credit to the devil when in reality it was me. Sometimes you open up those doors by flirting.

That's another sign of door openers, they can also be a sign of cheating, you know if you were very flirtatious.

Those are hoe tendencies. Especially when you're already taken. Don't nobody want no man or no woman especially if you in a relationship. I'm always flirting with everybody, there's a lot of attractive people in the world. That doesn't mean that you have to have everybody's attention, the only attention you should be seeking is attention from the one you're with.

Being in a relationship, your woman or your man should respect you whether they with you or without you. And when they're not with you, they should treat the situation as if you're still there, and vice versa. That's a hoe tendency. Whenever your woman or your man tells you to act totally different around company, when you're not even in their presence.

They act like they're afraid to say hi. Or make eye contact to the person they been talking to for several months, or even if they do know him, they act as if they don't know them, but behind your back they all in each other's face. As if they want to kiss, they know each other so well but they are distant the very second *you're around. Hoe tendencies, man understand this. Take heed to those that act different when you're around company, and when you're not around.*

Married women, married men

I slept with a married woman once, I must I say the thrill of it is what made it awesome. Now I knew better, and as well as she knew better, but it was like something that we both felt that it was a need.

We were highschoolers that used to flirt with one another all the time, and we both was virgins and we would talk to each other and say sexual things to each other, as if we were porn stars like we were really getting it in. Knowing neither one of us has ever had sex before. Almost 25 years later we met up. Started bringing up old times, and how we used to go at each other, and it was time to confront one another during the years about what was said. Mind you this is a married woman and I was a married man, we both were wrong, but that flesh, that lust, the desire took over.

She told her husband she was going to a business meeting or a trip. Basically I work third shift, so I got out as the house manager at the hotel. The very second she opened the door it was like wow, we haven't seen each other since 95 and it was crazy because it was like we were two kids again sneaking off to actually get a thing on. The thing is even though I was married, I was separated from my wife because she had already cheated, but I was still making moves as if I was a single man. For her on the other hand, she was happily married. It was just something that she felt she needed to scratch off of her list, which is something that she missed that we never got a chance to do, and the opportunity has now presented itself.

We sat on the bed and we talked for a good ten to fifteen minutes, until she just got fed up and said; did you come here to talk to me or come here to do what you said you was gonna do to me? And I replied to her. Suddenly this woman didn't hesitate to take off our clothes or nothing, no shame, simply planted the pillow on the floor, got settled a bit, and did what she knows to do. And she was actually very good at it.

She didn't like what she was doing, she loved what she was doing. While we were in motion, I said to myself in the process of doing this, what is running through her mind and what would her husband think? As far as he knows, she's on a business trip, a business meeting, but really the meeting was me, and her getting busy in the bed. After we were done it was like man, I can't believe it.

We finally done this after almost 25 years. On my way out the door she stopped and looked at me, and *she said; do you really have to go? I said not at the moment, but I got some things I have to do. She said; what can be more important than being here with me? Then we started all over again as if I just walked in the door, we repeated this three times. We had sex at least three times within the hour and 45 minutes I was there, and I thought to myself, does she even have a conscience to what was happening?*

We were both being sneaky and conniving. Should I say hoes, because I knew what I was doing I knew I was wrong, but she most definitely knew what she was doing, and she enjoyed it. And I said to her; man you don't feel no type of way? And she says; not really. I said; but aren't you happy? She responded, yes I'm happy, but I can finally say I finally felt you, and it was exactly what I expected, and if I have the opportunity I'll do it again. My mouth dropped like wow, the sex was so good and only so good because it was a thing. Should I say sex, it should've never happened, the thrill made it almost like the best sex that I've ever had because in reality, it was forbidden.

If it's ever too good to be true or just too darn good, It's not good for you. It's always like that to the point where anything that's not supposed to be touched. There's always something behind it, something that is too good to taste, it's always a consequence that you have to face. I learned my lesson with the exes and the jump offs, me being a hoe making decisions with a bitter of mind in a vulnerable heart, it's not healthy it's crazy.

Looking back on my life and all of the hearts I've broken and the people I disappointed and pain that I cost, and the people that looked up to me, and those that wasn't expecting me to move the way that I moved, all due to my brokenness. My mindset tripped and fell back into being something that I hated, and I fell into being something that hurt myself.

I picked up everything that was in me that I slept with. I picked up that don't care attitude, I can push on to the next really quick mentality, and with that, if you neglect and ignore me spirit, I'll go jump in the bed with the next. I learned to drop a few tears to get people to feel sorry for me just to get them in my bed.

People use all sorts of things and ways to get whatever it is that they want from you.

Sympathy, anger, pity, jealousy, anything to make you move the way that they want you to move. (manipulation)Now I'm not calling any of these women hoes, due to they are good women in a lot of ways, but the mentality was off the chain. Put it this way, some people are just meant to just be friends, but when you try to take it to another level it all ends.

In a relationship they have no morals, they value nothing about it or you. Especially if they have friends that are toxic as well. If your lover listens to his or her friends before they listen to you, and always taking advice from them and things just seem to get worse, you might as well cash it in.

You can't be in a relationship doing single things, it's all about respect and if she or he can't give you that, then you both don't need to be together. I was in love with a woman who claimed she loved me but was in lust with every guy she came encounter with. The very second our relationship got frustrated.

I was willing to work things but she wasn't. It was like once we broke up for some years and bumped into one another, she would tell me all the things she'd wished she would have done and how she wished we could start things all over, and I'd fall for it every time. She knew exactly what to do, a few tears and I miss you's and a blowjob. I was weaker than a baby bird when it came to that. She would ask me to pull out anywhere just to see it and I was so off, I would do it.

This woman had a hold on me tough due to she knew I really loved her. Let me see your...is all she had to say and in a split second of the moment she was sucking the soul out of me dry.

Sex is a powerful weapon to use against a man, a woman is very dangerous and have a power that a man would never possess.

Just like the married woman, my intentions were not to sleep with her, but something came over me to the point that I couldn't say no. The opportunity came and presented itself and I took it. I felt so bad because she had a good man and to this day, he has not a clue at all. Somethings you just have to keep buried for life, but God knows and sees all things and I vowed to never sleep with her again or another married woman period. Everything I went through was all a chain reaction. I hurt people that wanted something real out of a man.

However, I've never gotten anything real out of the women I tried to settle with.

Rule #1 Don't dump out the mess the last has dumped on you, unto the next. It's not fair to that person who possibly deserves a chance to have something nice for once in their lives.

Rule #2 Never compare your new to the last, even though you may see similarities, just always remember they aren't your ex.

Rule #3 Never keep secrets and never tell lies. keep everything all facts at 100%.

Rule #4 Never dwell on your past, it's okay to vent about it but don't vent as if you miss it.

Think highly of yourself as well, the bible says so as a man thinketh, so is he.

If you look at yourself as a hoe and think that explains why you move the way you do, don't even allow people to speak these things into your life.

Just because your mother, father, or even grandparents to whomever raised you didn't set you no type of example, doesn't mean you have to follow in their footsteps of not knowing any structure in a relationship. Some of us are the way we are due to seeing our mothers and fathers with many men and women in out our lives, and we pick up that trait of having many lovers or other things taken place in life.

It doesn't mean you have to be what and who someone says you are. I was a hoe all due to what I allowed myself to be. I took money from women; I sexed them for my own pleasure and out of revenge to get back at others. There was no limit to what I wouldn't do, especially being hurt and vulnerable. Sexing people I had no business with, in cars, driveways, truck stops and even behind banks and parks just to get one in.

I learned that just because a man or woman broke your heart and switched up on you, doesn't mean you gotta move like them, doesn't mean you gotta think like them. Because in reality all you were doing was opening up more doors, and you don't allow yourself to heal correctly, thinking like a hoe. Imagine falling in love with a Nymphomaniac. She's in love with the thought of you, but really she's in love with your sex. You put your heart into everything in that woman but all she could see you was as a tool. Imagine falling in love with a man and all he looks at you, is as a piece of meat, another hole to insert himself in to get off, that wants nothing to do with your heart, but everything to do with your body.

Some are like dogs, if you keep us outside our whole lives on a chain in the backyard, the very second we get free we don't go crazy, we gotta stick our tails to anything that will allow it to. A German Shepherd is not gonna stick to his own breed, he's gonna start his self in a poodle and a Pitbull and a lab, anything he can insert himself into. We are very similar to dogs but only if we are trained correctly. Women cheat because of neglect and hurt, men cheat because it looks good, because it's right there. We are curious on what the next woman may feel like and look like, but a woman she has to be hurt or she has to be feeling like she's neglected.

However, don't get me wrong, I know a few women to cheat just because they know they can, because of childhood issues and there was no counseling therapy. Or they just like to get their back broken in.

Think like a hoe 2

To protect their identity, I'm gonna use a false name but the situation is 100% facts. I went to school with this woman name Tamia Davis. However me and Tamia couldn't stand one another, so we'd pick with each other every day, we had something smart to say. I don't know what it was, maybe we liked each other while we were in high school but had a funny way of showing it. But me personally, I couldn't stand her. Long story short 2 1/2 years later I am now 17 and just lost my virginity.

I was on fire that summer and I just so happened to run across Tamia after not seeing her for two years in the projects, where we were now staying in. We got to chatting, talking about high school and what one another was doing and she just so happened to take an interest in one of my friends.

So I connected them, played the love connection. Mind you my homeboy was a minor at the time, he was 15 years old and she was 18, I really believe that she just wanted to play with his head and have him feeling in some type of way, because the very second she walked him to his door because he had a curfew, she came back to my house later on that night. Mind you this is the 90s, I want to say 98, we sat up and watched the movie called: booty calls, began to talk about the things that was taking place in the movie, then all of a sudden she says, what you know about that? It was a situation that took place in the movie sexually, and I replied: I know more than what you think. Then she jumps up as if she sat on a hot plate and ran outside and I thought to myself, what in the world was that? So I sat back down and I continued to watch the movie.

Moments later the door opens and shuts. I'm sitting here, she comes in complete silence and sits down. Then Tamia silently says: are you ready to go these 12 rounds? My reply was good. Tamia jumped up really aggressive in my face as I was sitting there, as if she wanted to fight. She went back home, because I noticed a change of clothes, because she had on some boy shorts the first time I've seen her, but she returned in a huge T-shirt with nothing on up under it but a Victoria's Secret negligee on. I must reminds you that I'm only 17 at the time and she was 18, but she's moving with the mindset of a 30 year old, she's gotta be experienced, which was what I thought, so we headed upstairs to my brothers room, because he had the bed and I had a couch in my room.

I'm going to the bathroom and freshen up for a minute while she's in the room, then I look into the mirror and look at myself striking a pose and I say, oh yeah, it's about to go down. I'm about to do some things to this girl she's never had done to her, not knowing that Tamia was very advanced. I came out of the bathroom and headed to the bedroom and there she was lying in the bed under the covers. In the dark I snatched the covers off of the bed off of her body and all I could see was chocolate brown skin from the moon light, coming in through the blinds from the window.

I'm thinking, oh yeah. Tamia replies, boy why did you snatch the covers off me like that? I responded: I don't know, I don't want no covers. She responded, it ain't like you can see anything, it's dark in here, and I replied: oh I can see you, trust and believe. One thing led to another, then there was a knock at the door, it was my mother. Quick, get in the closet. I said immediately to her.

Tamia jumps off the bed, grabs some stuff for the blanket and heads to the closet. My mom opens up the door and I plan like I was sleep. She said she just got off work early, saying that her back hurt, legs hurt, everything hurt. I responded, well mama do you want me to run you some bathwater? So I go into a room and running some bathwater to stall time, to give to Tamia time to escape.

71

I leave out my mother's bedroom so she can get herself ready for a bath and shut her door, headed to my brother's bedroom and open up the closet door and Tamia's not there. So, I headed downstairs to the bathroom that was down there and she was in there getting dressed. Meet me at my house, she says because she stayed right exactly behind me but a few doors down.

She leaves, so I wait about a good 15 minutes to get my mother settled. Mama!!I yell up the stairs and cry out, mama!!! I'll be back, I'm about to make a run real quick, she replies, well lock my door. And I head out. I leave the fence, ran over the hill and knocked on the door. She opens up the window and she says, meet me at the back door. So I go into the back door, the slider doors, and there she is.

My aunties upstairs, Tamia says, we gonna have to go into the bathroom. So we heading to the bathroom, when I stuck my toe on the corner of the wall, Tamia says, damn boy you going to wake everybody up. Come on. We close the bathroom door and continued where we left off, from the toilet to the sink, to the wall, two black rabbits going at it.

The very next day, guess who shows up at my house? My homeboy. Mind you I just hooked them up yesterday. What's good bro? He says as he's picking me up over here. We supposed to go to the carnival later on. I was like that's what's up, while the things that was running through my mind at that time was, man you just don't have a clue what I just did to your new girl just seven hours ago. Tamia comes over as if nothing took place or even happened, gave me some damn chill for a minute with her new boyfriend Mohammed, then they left.

The crazy thing is that they went to the carnival and afterwords went to their house and she slept with him, then later on that night came back and jumped in the bed with me. This went on for several months, of me sleeping with this woman. Until one day she found out that he lied about a woman that he slept with that was way before her. I guess that was her excuse to break up with him to continue to sleep with me, poor kid, you know what I'm saying? I mean he already didn't know that I was sleeping with her behind his back, and then I actually was sleeping with her before he started.

Mohammed cries out, I didn't touch that girl in four years, please don't break up with me I love you! I'm on the side laughing hysterically, while she was in the back explaining to him why she didn't want him anymore. You lied to me; you told me you didn't sleep with Tiana. It was the past! Replied Mohammad. It was before you! As he cried out, Tamia walked away from him and said it was over, Mohammed walked away with a broken heart. One of my good friends that was with us, that knew everything that I was doing, looked at me and said, Rick you might as well tell him. I looked at him and said Hank, I don't know, it was all funny to me, but I had to tell him.

Mohammed there's some things I gotta tell you, I started off. Mohammed replied with tears running down his face. I said to him: bro, she wasn't good for you anyway, besides I've been sleeping with her since the first day I hooked you guys up. Mohammed said angrily, what you fool?! You can't be serious! I laughed and replied, man I slept with her the very moment she walked you home that night. So pick your head up and push on, is what I told him. He experienced his first heartbreak and me myself, I continued to keep sleeping with Tamia.

Some friend that I was, I really didn't think anything was wrong with it at the time. All I cared about was what I wanted. Trust me, I got it back with many wolves dressed in sheep's clothing. It's a terrible feeling to think that you're in love with someone, and it turns out that you don't even know them like you thought you did.

Wolves in sheep's clothing

Have you ever gone to bed with someone and woke up and somebody different was in it? This is so crazy, I went to bed with someone that I thought I truly loved, that I would of probably gave my left lung to in order for them to survive, but woke up to a totally complete different character. She was insecure, she was mean and you never knew what she was going to do, the very second you woke up every day. She was always accusing me of other women, always accusing me that I was stepping out or I thought about somebody, and what I learned from this is that a person that's so quick to accuse you of something most likely..

A they've done it already

B they're thinking about it

C they're already in a position of doing it and just hope that you ain't doing it before them

It's crazy how we make seasonal people in our lives permanent people in our lives, which explains why those relationships in those things never work. You can take the hoe out the hood, but you can't take the hood out the hoe. He or she is going to transition themselves to whatever they feel you want them to be to get you, but once they are comfortable and you are comfortable, that's when the mask will fall off the face and you will see the scale of skin. These are some of the things that run through the mind of man.

I'm a do whatever it takes to get you even if it means not being myself, I will be whatever it takes to taste you even if it means I gotta season myself with something that is not of me. We will cry fake tears to the point, stack lies on top of lies to the point, we will actually start to believe our own lie depending on how and what it is.

A woman will pretty much do the same especially if you were a provider, she will sex you, cook for you be everything that she feels you want her to be, just to be with you. I consider this also a wolf in sheep's clothing.

We need to get the mindset of never chasing but attract, however there's nothing wrong with chasing but knowing what you're chasing is to make sure you're not chasing an illusion. Because there's all kinds of snakes out there that are not who they say they are.

Understand this, people and clearly everybody wants somebody to call their own, but everyone's not going to tolerate the mess that you dish out. Some people like to say I love being alone, and they choose to be alone, bull crap. To me some people are alone because aint no one going to put up with their mess. However they will never see that. Don't no one want no loud mouth I'm in control I gotta blast you out in public type of woman, and don't no one want no I don't want a job stay at home but can hang out all night type of lazy man.

Sometimes you don't see this in the people you fall in love with until you move in with them. Then once your heart is inclined with them, a whole new person is emerging out.

Even though you may love that person or used to love that person, once you part from them it could never go back to the way it used to be no matter how much you try. Because certain people would never go back to being what they used to be in your life, and you just have to accept the fact that they no longer exist. They gonna be who they always been, and that's not you, so why convert over to it.

Be The sheep in wolves clothing not the wolf in sheep's clothing, you'd rather be the sheep in the clothing of a wolf. Why play the fool when you can be *the sheep, just like the wolf, and out think the person that's claiming they love you, but why even bother, stay away from it.*

Why think like a hoe when you can think more civilized as a person with morals with value, it's not about always getting over with somebody or seeing what you can gain, or draining someone's energy and waste someone's time and deceiving someone, is it all really worth it? If you want a good woman or a good man, position yourself to receive a good woman or a good man. How can you can expect a 10 when you're really a 4? You can't expect God to bless you with a good woman or a good man if your filled with mess.

You get a lot of women that aren't feminine enough, sexual enough, and expect and want a man to cater to them at every need. However, you get men that aren't compassionate enough aren't manly enough and expect the woman to perform all of her duties, when he can't even keep a job or get a job, matter fact keep his penis in his pants and not share it with the world.

Alpha female is not going to stand for that type of mess, an alpha female is going to hold her own, she's gonna take care of business she's not gonna claim she's some boss bitch, she's not going to even hold that type of title to herself. An alpha female is gonna take care of her kids, if she has anything going for herself, she's going to take care of her business, she's gonna recognize the real or she will drop you like a bad habit the very second you show a sign of weakness. She'll be your friend but as your woman, never. A lot of people aren't really hoes, they just have a hoe mentality because they was never taught. They make moves not even knowing the moves that they make shapes their character, and they wonder why they attract what they attract, to continue hurting themselves and hurting others do to their hoe mentality.

An alpha male, he is strong, confident, has no insecurities, he wants a woman that can line up pretty much to his expectations and he can line up to hers. He's about his business and will take care of her children as his own, if she has children. An alpha male is not going to let anything cross his boundaries, especially when it comes to his woman. This alpha male will have his own job his own money, he will be looking for a woman that can bring something to the table, because two heads is better than one, but if he got it all and can take care of it all, he will as long as that alpha woman can hold down the fort while he's out making bread.

A lot of the times these Alpha females get stuck with these hyena hoes, and the alpha males get stuck with these hyena hoes. They're savages, seeking to devour anything in its path, they don't want to hunt on their own, they hunt in packs. They'll sit and wait till you're vulnerable and lonely, then come in and devour you.

People love to kick you when you're down so when you heal, you learn. The new you need to make people feel intimidated because you are new. You're no longer the old you, but you are the new and improved you.

I know that people are gonna say, oh man he's talking about women being hoes. No I'm not, it's kind of funny how a man can sleep with several women and not be labeled, and if he is labeled he's considered a player, a king or a pimp. And other names that appraisal for what he's done. However, if a woman does the same thing she's labeled a hoe, a slut, a chicken head, a jump off, all these crazy names to degrade women, especially our black women. We all are in search for this true love, that one special true love, we just don't know and don't realize what it is until we find God, and that's when we find our true love within our true selves.

Anytime you find somebody that said that they love you and they distract you from doing right, and distract you from God, they most definitely aren't for you. When you're seeking God and trying to go one direction and the goal is to please him and not man, that's when you'll find that true you. And that identity that you've been searching for will come to an end. Upgrade you for you, not for nobody else, change for you and nobody else, please you first and nobody else.

Your identity has been finessed for way too long, you've been living in somebody else's shadow for way too long, change your way of thinking like a hoe, it's got you drifting, shifting, changing faces.

The side chick/side dude

Why is it that it's the good women that get overlooked and hoes are now in?

It seems as if the men now want those half-dressed women with the breast hanging out and the booty bouncing all over the media, who brags on how they don't have any gag reflex, or etc. gets the good life with the good men.

While the good women are at home washing clothes, making sure the house is all good, the food is cooked, and all while their man is out hoeing loving and being everything to everyone.

Why are the good guys overlooked?

The men that go to work and comes home from the 9 to 5 whose eyes never wander, who take care of their children. That says that they're going be in one place and that's where they're going to be. The good guys are overlooked, but the guys that end up with the good girls be the ones who flash their money, have more than one side chick, don't come home at night or late in the a.m.

I see this a lot, in my experience I've seen with both of my exes is that they want to chase, feed, and control a brother. I see men and women who chase and want people who can't really take care of themselves, they want their man or woman to depend completely on them.

However, if the woman is independent or male, they'll possibly be cheated on. Due to the fact they'll feel you are not in need. That's when they'll fall in the role of playing the victim, to step out and open a door, and tell all the negative things about you to get the other person to feel a certain way about them.

Us men only cheat due to lust, we can possibly be in love with the woman we cheat on, however women have different reasons to why they cheat, but mainly it's out of emotion. In other words, it's pretty much over when your woman cheats. You can have a huge bank account, ain't no money in the world going to make her come back to you, and if she does, she won't be loyal at all, especially if the money runs out.

Guys use women all the time in this way. I see guys play all day but as soon as income tax goes around or the seasons change, it's on to the next, and it doesn't matter how the woman looks, she can be broke, but if she has a place to stay, he's on her. But money plays a big role in a lot of things. I seen guys cheat on their woman due to how fat the next woman butt is, or just by word of mouth how good she can give oral sex, etc. We can be dogs to the maximum, as long as she has a hole we jumping in her. We take that chance of losing everything, our wife, our children, and our home, all due to a one nightstand.

7 seconds of pleasure

7 seconds of pleasure is how long an orgasm is, 7 seconds. I can honestly say in my opinion that women are much stronger than us in this area. They're not going to cheat unless they really don't care that it's over. Unless they just feel they don't have too much to risk. Some just don't care, and they are good with being the side chick. The side chick does everything so much better, she listens, sexes you different, but just so right, and it's the same way with the side dude. You can tell us your secrets, we fold you right, we treat you right, we be pretty much everything your man or woman is not.

What people don't realize is that the side chick and side dude job isn't hard at all, due to the fact they'll never get or see the real you. That woman or man that's loyal to you knows the real you. You are the one who's putting up with his or her attitude, the real tears, the family, everything that goes on at home, all the frustrations. While the side chick or dude is doing nothing but listening and comforting. Who you love with compassion, which is just sex, due to they don't really care. They are out for the cheap thrill. They're getting all the compassion while you're at home in tears breaking down, wondering but knowing, and feeling things are not right.

Some people just can't get their own woman or own man, they target someone else's. Which is the thrill, when in reality they don't really want you. Cheating is never worth it. Why break up your home? When you could just work it out, but you give it all up for a one-night stand and damage things for life? The side dude only wants one thing and that's what's in your pants and to prove that he's better than the man that you've chosen. It also makes him feel very good to know that you have a man but in reality, he knows you could never be his woman, because you're one that he'll never look at as loyal.

I should've known that when I got with my second wife, she was dating a dude for some months and when I got with her, she dropped him like a bad habit. She was coming to see me on the down low, and eventually I ended up with her and married her.

I came from being her husband, to being her side dude twice, which is crazy, and both times I ended up being the jump off, coming back to her. She got another guy coming back-and-forth to her, while having yet another guy.

It came to the point that she became the side chick as well. She was the side chick though, who fell in love with the main dude that ended up facing karma in the end.

The crazy thing is, I once had a girl named Keisha. I mean Keisha was everything that a guy would want in a woman, she cooked she cleaned, she did everything. But I also found myself with a side chick named Sue. Sue did everything as well, but did it better, even though she knew I was attracted to Keisha and that was who I was with. Sue knew that I was with Keisha, I had a woman. However, me and Sue was just cool. But once I stopped returning her phone calls and stopped calling her as much as I used to for comfort, things began to change. Sue knew my wants and needs, even though we had never had sex before, but when the time presented itself, Sue blew my mind. I didn't know if she was in competition with Keisha, or with any woman that I've ever spoken to her about.

She sucked on me like a supernatural porn star, I've never had sex like that in my life. I did some things that I've never done before, and I thought I've done it all. Besides I was in a relationship for 15 years, but this thing that was happening was something different. I was going back-and-forth from Sue to Keisha, from Sue to Keisha, to eventually I chose Sue, and the consequences I had to suffer were great.

Because Sue had everything to offer when it came to sex, but she couldn't hold a conversation whenever she got frustrated. When it was time to take care of business, we spoke two different languages.

The funny thing about Sue was that she did exactly to me what I did to Keisha. Nights I would go to work, she would slip off with a friend to meet up with guys. Conversations with guys about our personal business and the trials that we went through, to eventually she started inviting the guys over to her house, which I stayed with her, and eventually brought us to an end. And soon after, she moved the guy in and I was yesterday's news. This is something else, it's like a pyramid effect, because he turned around and did her dirty as well.

I got back exactly what I did to Keisha, sad case being the side dude, falling in love with a side chick, can't win. Because first of all God doesn't bless no mess.

Some of us are watering plants that refuse to grow, and if they won't grow, don't continue to keep watering them. Dig that thing from the root and go on with your life. Because if you never healed from any of the things that abused you, that cut you, that hurt you, then you'll bleed on everybody around you that never cut you. They never stuck you, they never even put their hands on you, it will cause them to be toxic and infected by you.

Don't take what someone else has done to you, to cause you to change and dump it out on somebody else. Allow yourself to heal. I was once that hoe, that abuser, that heartbreaker, everything that I wrote in this book was all me.

I was the victim who became the villain, then the villain who became the victim.

Instead of changing for the better, I changed for the worse. It was devastating how the first love left me for some dude that uses drugs and lives at his mother's house, and sold drugs and used his own mother. She left her whole household to downgrade. I guess like they say, when a woman's fed up, she's fed up. You would think they would at least upgrade, set the expectations high.

I thought I was upgrading when I went onto the next, but the only difference was when she would work, she left me for a drunk who stayed with his parents in the basement of their home, that didn't even have a license or a car to get them from point A to point B. I guess they either like being in control or being controlled, instead of somebody who put them on the same level or had higher expectations for them. You can see all the potential you want in a person, but if they don't see it in themselves then it's pointless. It took a while for me to understand the reason why women use me up and the reason why some guys will use you up as well. It's only because you draw people that need you, and not people that can feed you.

We find ourselves dumbing down to people that are comfortable in their situations, and once we pull them out, they end up seeing a New World. But eventually they go back into their own world or bring their old world into your new, and contaminate that all over to the point they're back in their comfort zone.

Always remember that you don't owe nobody anything. You don't have to give nobody no opportunity to meet the new you, let them see the new you, it'll be a privilege for you to even give them conversation, especially if you dealt with them before, it could be as simple as a hi and goodbye.

Understand this, there's many people out there that don't even like you and haven't even heard your side of the story. And if you have good intentions, you don't lose people ever, they lose you.

If it takes for someone to cheat on you, to abuse you, to go jump in the bed with somebody else to realize what they had once they did these things on you, man they don't ever deserve another chance. They'll be lucky to get a 'how are you doing?' Value yourself more than that, don't allow yourself to be used ever again, sex is something that you will not let overpower you. You don't have to tolerate bull crap from anybody to be loved.

Learn to recognize people's intentions and motivations and see through the smoke screens where people surround their actions and understand people. Their hidden motives are the greatest piece of knowledge that you could ever inquire about a person, is what I've learned.

Not everyone you lose is a loss, unless it's yourself. Whenever a person loses you, it really sucks to be them, because they really never knew what they had when they lost you.

I ask myself this a lot and not to be funny, but did I fall in love with somebody that I was supposed to just bang? Somebody that should've just been a one night stand? Which explains why I'm in the situation that I am in. We all have had or have a little hoe in us. But progress is all about change, you can remain the same and you can go on living your life, attracting things which you don't want and it's not who you are. You can fix it and you can make a difference. Don't continue to think like no hoe.

The weirdest thing ever told to me came from my ex-mother-in-law. I was 25 years old around the time, if not 23. She told me (head) in other words oral sex, could either make a home or break up a home. All the conversations we used to have was very intriguing, but yet weird, and it all made me kind of curious to know all about an older woman.

However, we never had any sexual encounters, but I did used to mess with my imagination, and I thought to myself, this is not good, I'm thinking about sleeping with somebody's grandmother, matter fact my children's grandmother and how disgusting. But the way she used to talk in the stories, she used to tell me things that would cause any man to think the things that I was thinking.

My thing was she was either trying to set me up or suck me up. That sexual spirit is a strong hold on anybody. My mind was so contaminated I didn't know whether to go forward, backwards, sideways or whatever. That's why you must keep a clear mind and be careful of who you hang around with. I have family members that were trying to tempt me to get her to perform oral sex on me, to beat her up to see how far I could take it, but it was something in me that would not allow me to do it. So one day I told her we no longer can have these type of conversations again, besides it was her doing all the talking, I would just listen.

I had a hoe mentality with a hoe mindset. I used to be able to picture women with their clothes off, as they were talking to me, picture the sexual sounds they would make as if I was having sex with them. I would plot and plan on going over to women houses that would just wanna kick it with me, and play innocent as if I'm not into sexing with them, just to get them to come home with me.

I was that nasty individual that will get women to dare me to do things, just so I can show them my private area, and once they asked to see my private area, I would dare them to do things with it. I would manipulate them and control the mind so that I could control the situation, and next thing you know I was spending the night.

I never matured in situations like this. My maturity didn't process through the years. It started processing when I started recognizing the damage that I was allowing to take place in my life. It was hard shaking off some of those demons that I picked up from the lovers and jump offs that I had.

I learned to never ever waste your time trying to explain yourself to someone who's committed to being disloyal to you, and who misunderstands you.

Change your way of thinking, don't accept and take in what others say about you, and most definitely never convert to what hurt you and what you despise.

You don't have to think like a hoe.

But think like the queen and king you say you are.

Stay tuned for these upcoming titles by Ricky Boone

Pillow Talk 2-Voodoo

Guns and Butter

About The Author

Born in Saginaw Michigan but raised in Grand Rapids Michigan, Ricky Boone discovered his passion for writing when he was 14 years old. He attempted to write his first book based on his love for movies.

"I've always seen part two and three even before they were created. However, I watched a movie called 'Under the Cherry Moon' by Prince, and the poetry he wrote in the movie inspired me, and I've been hooked ever since."

Author Ricky Boone links into many poets such as Desiree Renea, a poet that was dedicated into ministry in the church. She introduced him, and he stood up in front of the congregation. Later on, he started following Black Ice, which was another poet as well that gave Ricky Boone the push he needed.

Afterwards he joined a group on Facebook called The Inner Circle, which was ran by Kesha Murphy and king Judah. Both were erotic and love poets who asked Ricky to collaborate with them, which sparked a flame that drew him into a totally new audience. This eventually caused Ricky Boone to start writing out his emotions and experiences. "Through my marriages, whether it was on a positive or negative level, I figured why give up on love; because it hasn't given up on me. I started to desire certain things, wanting to share with that special person, and thought well...I know I can't be the only one who desires these things. By the end of my divorce in 2017, which I thought would have broken me, I learned to channel that pain into what I wanted in a woman, and how I wanted her to treat me. And that was the birth of my first book, pillow talk."

Now, Author Ricky Boone has taken his success to the next level, in urban erotica and drama, with his books: Juice Box, and The Bouquet and his self-help book: Jezebel's Kiss.

To learn more about Author Ricky Boone and his creatively written works and upcoming books, visit the publishing website.

www.AJBPublishiing.com

www.ingramcontent.com/pod-product-compliance
Lightning Source LLC
Chambersburg PA
CBHW071101090426

42737CB00013B/2423